CELLO, BASS

From The Baroque To The 20th Century

Classical Trios for All

Playable on ANY THREE INSTRUMENTS
or any number of instruments in ensemble

WILLIAM RYDEN

TABLE OF CONTENTS

The Village Maiden ....Jean Philippe Rameau (1683-1764) 3

Rosamunde ....Franz Schubert (1797-1828) 4
(Entr'Acte No. 2, D.797)

German Dance, WoO 13, No. 2 ....Ludwig van Beethoven (1770-1827) 6

Ländler *(Austrian Dance)*...............................Franz Schubert (1797-1828) 8

Romance ....Robert Schumann (1810-1856) 8
(Album For The Young, Op. 68, No. 19)

Rigaudon ....Louis Claude Daquin (1694-1772) 10

Passacaglia *("Dido And Aeneas")*....................Henry Purcell (1659-1695) 11

Trio in F *(Minuet, BWV 820)* ....Johann Sebastian Bach (1685-1750) 12

Andantino ....Daniel Gottlob Türk (1750-1813) 13

Canon...Antonio Caldara (1670-1736) 14

Waltz *("Eugene Onegin")* ....Piotr Ilyich Tchaikovsky (1840-1893) 16

March ....Erik Satie (1866-1925) 18
("La Diva De L'Empire")

Minuet, Hob. XVI, No. 5 ....Joseph Haydn (1732-1809) 20

Waltz in B Minor, Opus 39, No. 11 ....Johannes Brahms (1833-1897) 22

Adagio..Arcangelo Corelli (1653-1713) 24
(Sonata, Opus 1, No. 3)

INSTRUMENTATION

EL96139 - Piano/Conductor, Oboe
EL96140 - Flute, Piccolo
EL96141 - B♭ Clarinet, Bass Clarinet
EL96142 - Alto Saxophone
            (E♭ Saxes and E♭ Clarinets)
EL96143 - Tenor Saxophone
EL96144 - B♭ Trumpet, Baritone T.C.

EL96145 - Horn in F
EL96146 - Trombone,
            Baritone B.C., Bassoon, Tuba
EL96147 - Violin
EL96148 - Viola
EL96149 - Cello/Bass
EL96150 - Percussion

Editor: Thom Proctor
Cover: Dallas Soto

EL96149

ALPHABETICAL CONTENTS

Adagio ....Arcangelo Corelli   (1653-1713) 24
(Sonata, Opus 1, No. 3)

Andantino ....Daniel Gottlob Türk   (1750-1813) 13

Canon ....Antonio Caldara   (1670-1736) 14

German Dance, WoO 13, No. 2 ....Ludwig van Beethoven   (1770-1827) 6

Ländler *(Austrian Dance)* ....Franz Schubert   (1797-1828) 8

Passacaglia *("Dido And Aeneas")* ....Henry Purcell   (1659-1695) 11

March ....Erik Satie   (1866-1925) 18
("La Diva De L'Empire")

Minuet, Hob. XVI, No. 5 ....Joseph Haydn   (1732-1809) 20

Rigaudon ....Louis Claude Daquin   (1694-1772) 10

Romance ....Robert Schumann   (1810-1856) 8
(Album For The Young, Op. 68, No. 19)

Rosamunde ....Franz Schubert   (1797-1828) 4
(Entr'Acte No. 2, D.797)

Trio in F *(Minuet, BWV 820)* ....Johann Sebastian Bach   (1685-1750) 12

The Village Maiden ....Jean Philippe Rameau   (1683-1764) 3

Waltz *("Eugene Onegin")* ....Piotr Ilyich Tchaikovsky   (1840-1893) 16

Waltz in B Minor, Opus 39, No. 11 ....Johannes Brahms   (1833-1897) 22

WILLIAM RYDEN was born in New York City and is a life-long resident of Forest Hills, New York. He received his advanced musical training at The American Conservatory of Music in Chicago and at the Mannes College of Music in New York. The diversity of his composing ranges from solos to orchestra works, in both vocal and instrumental music. Since 1982 he has received 25 grants from the Meet-the-Composer Foundation. His numerous compositions and arrangements have been published by various prominent educational and performance music publishers.

THE VILLAGE MAIDEN

CELLO / BASS

JEAN PHILLIPE RAMEAU
(1683-1764)

EL96149

ROSAMUNDE
Entr'acte No. 2, D.797

FRANZ SCHUBERT
(1797-1828)

GERMAN DANCE

WoO 13, No. 2

LUDWIG VAN BEETHOVEN
(1770-1827)

Allegro moderato

D.C. al Fine

LÄNDLER
Austrian Dance

FRANZ SCHUBERT
(1797-1828)

ROMANCE
Album for the Young, Opus 68, No. 19

ROBERT SCHUMANN
(1810-1856)

RIGAUDON

Allegro moderato

LOUIS CLAUDE DAQUIN
(1694-1772)

PASSACAGLIA
"Dido and Aeneas"

HENRY PURCELL
(1659-1695)

TRIO in F
Minuet, BWV 820

JOHANN SEBASTIAN BACH
(1685-1750)

ANDANTINO

DANIEL GOTTLOB TÜRK
(1750-1813)

Andantino con tenerezza (tenderly)

CANON

ANTONIO CALDARA
(1670-1736)

★ Optional 8va

WALTZ
"Eugen Onegin"

PIOTR ILYICH TCHAIKOVSKY
(1840-1893)

MARCH
"La Diva de L'empire"
(1919)

ERIK SATIE
(1866-1925)

2. Play second time only.

Minuet

Hob. XVI, No. 5

JOSEPH HAYDN
(1732-1809)

WALTZ
in B minor
Opus 39, No. 11

JOHANNES BRAHMS
(1833-1897)

Moderately fast waltz

ADAGIO
Sonata, Opus 1, No. 3

ARCANGELO CORELLI
(1653-1713)

Adagio